A Time for Every Purpose

BETTY ISLER

Concordia
Publishing House
St. Louis

Copyright © 1985 Concordia Publishing House
3558 S. Jefferson Avenue, St. Louis, MO 63118-3968
Manufactured in the United States of America

Library of Congress Cataloging-in-Publication Data

Isler, Betty, 1915-
    A time for every purpose.

    1. Women—Prayer-books and devotions—English. I. Title.
BV4844.I84 1986   242'.643   85-16798
ISBN 0-570-03986-X

1 2 3 4 5 6 7 8 9 10 PP 94 93 92 91 90 89 88 87 86 85

A Time for
Every Purpose

Contents

TIME OUT

TIME IN

Adult Education

Lord,
My need for You
Is unceasing;
My thirst is never
Entirely quenched;
My hunger
For Your teaching
Never quite sated.

Furthermore, Lord,
The lesson material
Never becomes
Outdated.

From the Heart

Lord, Thank You for allowing me
The freedom and ease
Of informality
When I speak with You.

Thank You for knowing
That such familiarity
Is not disrespectful
But comes only
From the footstool
Of humility.

Displaced Person

Lord,
Sometimes I think
I am nothing more than
A little old lady
In corrective shoes
Who talks to herself
A lot.

I live in the
Wrong time slot
In a plastic world
Where the mother tongue
Is computerese
And when people speak
I do not even know
What game they
Are playing.

How thankful I am, Lord,
That I can always escape
Into Your Word,
Where You talk to me
And I know what You
Are saying.

Unexpected Blessing

Lord,
You continually delight me,
Answering my prayers
The way You do,
In Your own way,
Always to perfection . . .

And usually when
I am looking in
Another direction!

The Guest

Lord,
Every woman wonders
How it would be
If You suddenly
Dropped in for dinner.

Marthas that we are,
We dream of bringing out
The best lace cloth,
The good china,
The crystal goblets,
Then somehow coming up
With a menu worthy of You—
Possibly the next
Pillsbury Bake-off
All-time winner!

With my luck
You will arrive
The night we are having
Warm-overs of some
Dreary kind.

Lord,
Will You mind?

13

Promise

Lord,
I accept this
As one of Your truths,
Although it is not
Always clear:

After the storm
A rainbow will
Appear.

Prime Time

Lord,
No matter the hour,
Or the date,
No matter how late
Or how long
I have been gone,

When I tune in to
Your channel,
You are always
ON!

Lesson

Lord,
I am slowly learning
How to forgive,
But forgetting
Is something else.

It takes so long
To erase an image
That remains constant.

Yet You, Lord,
Not only forgive
But forget in
An instant!

15

The Least Ones

Lord,
I am one of Your
Middle-of-the-road people.
We mosey along
In our same old
Mediocre rut,
Without fanfare
Or dash,
Never doing anything
Sensational,
Never making much
Of a splash.
Our simple achievements
Seem hardly worth
Trying for.

The MIRACLE is . . .
You found us worth
Dying for!

Kitchen Wisdom

I have learned
That a woman can often
Divert a threatening
Marital storm
Merely by producing
A fresh-baked apple pie
And serving it
Warm.

Unfinished . . .

Lord,
Each night
My evening prayers
Seem to grow longer.

There are
So many friends
For whom I ask
Your help
That I must confess
I sometimes fall asleep
Before reaching the
End of the list.

Lord,
Forgive me
And continue to bless
All those souls
Whose names
I missed.

Refresher Course

My neighbor
Is taking a course
In "self-awareness."
She claims she needs
To find herself,
That life is stale.
She is looking for
Something new.

I wish I could tell her
She would feel
Renewed and refreshed
If she would first
Look for You.

19

Revelation

This woman,
So aloof and cool,
Whom I thought I did not like,
Suddenly opened a tiny window
Onto her soul with one,
Offhand, unguarded remark . . .
And through it I could see
Her own long, dark
Corridors of fear
Into which she
Privately descends.

Now I know
We will be friends.

Speaker for the Day

Lord,
I really want to
Witness for You.
Really want to
Spread the good news.
So Lord, please,
Help me with these
Spaghetti knees!

Sunday Morning

I sit here
In last year's coat,
Feeling ordinary
And humdrum . . .

Until I remember
We do not come
Into Your house
To be seen
But to worship
And learn . . .

And You do not care
What we wear.

Blueprint

We mortals take a given space,
Build walls around it,
Divide it into
Rigid compartments
And call it
Structural security.

You, Lord,
Take all of space
And without any
Visible trace
Of framework
Give us eternal security,
And all the lines
Fall in pleasant places.

Pattern for Living

Lord,
It is really so simple
It is almost absurd . . .

All I have to do
Is take You
At Your Word.

Self-image

Some days, Lord,
I do not feel very important.
I do not feel that I am
A person of much substance.
I do not exactly
Cut a wide swath
Through life.

Some people,
Meeting me again,
Do not even remember me,
Which leaves me
At a loss

Until

I remember how
Important I am to You . . .
So important that You made
The supreme sacrifice
For me at Calvary,
On a cross.

No Hits, No Runs

Lord,
If life is really a game,
As they say,
Then I played poorly today;
Had my eye off the ball
Too often, made
Mistakes galore.

Thank You, Lord
For never
Keeping score!

Regrets

Lord,
Help me to
Control my tongue.
I react too quickly,
And speak carelessly.

Help me to avoid
The bitter taste
Of hurtful words
That cannot be erased.

When a Grown Child Hurts

Lord,
I cannot wrap her
In that shred of a blanket
And rock away the pain.

I cannot give her a cookie
And a glass of milk
To make her smile again.

I cannot kiss
That wounded heart
And cover it with
A bandage.

But I can help her
To manage . . .
To see it through
By turning to You.

Pearls of Wisdom

From the advantage
Of all my years
I could give such
Jewels of advice
To my grandchildren
If they would just
Listen to me.

Are You smiling, Lord?
You, who have
The same problem with me
So consistently?

Ready to Wear

True faith
Is such an adaptable garment.
The label does not read
Large, Medium
Or Small.

No alterations
Are ever necessary.
Just one size
Fits all.

Small Time

I wish I would not think
About so many little things.
I fill every nook and cranny
Of my mind with trivia,
Spend too much time
Fretting over details
And inconsequentials.

I think I need to have
A garage sale
To clear out the clutter
In my head
And make room for
Essentials.

Small Pleasures

This is such a dark
And dreary day,
Wet and bleak.
I plod through my errands,
Head down, trying
Not to mind.

Crossing the
Rain-slick street,
A patch of oil
Reflects a bit of sky
And spreads a rainbow
At my feet.

On such a day,
I take what beauty
I can find.

Low Boiling Point

Lord,
I know I am
Too easily irritable.
I flare up too quickly,
Speak out recklessly
And wind up having
To eat my own words,
(Often indigestible.)

Lord,
Help me to calm down,
To be more considerate
And less combustible.

Illumination

Lord,
It has at long last
Occurred to me
That I cannot pray for
Enlightenment from You
Until I lift up
The corners of
My own mind
And allow the fresh air
Of Your wisdom
To ventilate the
Dark crevices.

Now,
In the revealing glare
Of Your Light,
I see things
From a new angle
And recognize roadblocks
Of my own making
I did not know
Were there.

Primary Lesson

Lord,
Your Way is really so easy
And so elementary,
That frequently
The very simplicity
Goes unappreciated.

Sometimes I think
We try to make it
Complicated.

Foreign Language

Lord,
Today when I visit
My grandchildren
They use a lingo and
Expressions I have
Never before heard.

I will not worry,
However, if they keep
Your name as a
Household word.

The Source

Once I was timid,
Fearful among other people,
Unsure of my welcome.

Now I walk and talk
With assurance
And people think
I have found new
Confidence in myself.

I have new confidence,
It is true,
But I found it
In You.

Planning Committee

Lord,
I feel so out of place
In this group of
Younger church women.
I don't really
Belong here.

They are so
Fresh-faced and eager,
Full of new approaches
And enthusiasm.
I feel old and tired,
Like a Rent-a-Dent
In a parking lot
Of new sports cars.

But we open
With a prayer
And pool our ideas,
Each one listening
To the other.

And You know what, Lord?
I really do
Belong here!

Hear Our Prayer

Lord,
Of all Your comforts,
The sweetest,
By far,
Is what a good
Listener
You are.

Quality Control

Lord,
I need help
In leveling out
My days.

I am not consistent
In my service
To You.
I blow hot and cold
In witnessing
And praise.

Lord,
Forgive me these
Uneven interludes
When I lose direction.

Were You a less
Compassionate Master
I would never
Pass inspection.

True Value

Lord,
How merciful
That You do not require
Coupons for the
Marvelous offer of
Your Love.

What's more,
You never designate
An expiration date.

Personal Therapy

Lord,
With You as my counselor
There is no
Preliminary sparring
As in a group,
No need to establish
My identity,
No judgment by peers,
No spilling of my soul
To a roomful of
Alien faces.

With You, Lord,
It is always on
A one-to-One basis.

Honesty

Lord,
Sometimes I think
I am too often an
Armchair Christian.

I talk a strong faith,
But have days when
I knuckle under
To fears.

I sing of knowing You
As unutterable joy,
Yet often give way
To tears.

Lord,
You, who are so
Everlastingly steadfast,
Whose unwavering strength
I seek.
Help me to
Fit my actions
To the words I speak.

Insufficient Funds

The day the bank statements
Arrive in the mail
With their deadly figures
Which never match mine,
I become automatically,
Symptomatically,
Pyschosomatically
SICK!

Lord,
Where was I
When Your committee of angels
Passed out skills in
Arithmetic?

Street Scene

Lord,
Whatever the situation,
However sticky or unpretty,
No matter what complicated
Problem needs to be solved . . .

You are never
Just a spectator,
Fading into the background.
When things get down
To the nitty-gritty
You always come forward,
ASKING to be
Involved!

Support System

Lord,
The broken bones
Have mended.
I have put away
The walker and the cane
And no longer limp
(Very much.)

But You and I know
That You are my
Invisible crutch.

No Explanation Necessary

Lord,
Sometimes I find myself
In situations that are
So complex,
So confusing,
So muddled,
They addle my brain . . .

But I can always
Come to You for help
Without having
To explain.

Postage Due

Lord,
If I were ever required
To make a package
Of all my blessings,
Including every
Single one,
It couldn't be done!

No matter how
I bend, staple, or
Fold them,
No container
Could hold them.

The Marathoner

Lord,
I am truly
"Over the hill."
Like an old car,
Machinery rusting out,
Engine performance
Below par.

However,
As the Master Mechanic,
Somehow You keep me
In running condition
With Your periodic,
Incredible, spiritual
Overhauls.
Just one more
Of those miracles
You so quietly render.

But Lord,
On that last little hill,
I think I may have
Lost a fender!

The Heaping

Lord,
You do not measure out
Your gifts by
The teaspoon
Or the cup,
Do not confine Your blessings
To a prescribed recipe
Or limit the amount.

In all Your giving
There is a fullness
Beyond count.

The Impossible Task

I went to bed vowing
I could not
Do it.

This morning
You showed me
How to get
Through it.

The Ratings

Lord,
I am not even going
To ask You
How I would rate
As a Christian
On a scale of
One to ten.

I am glad You
Do not stoop
To such nonsense.

Besides, It would not be
Very smart,
Because there are days
I might not even
Show up on
Your chart.

Call for Action

Faith
Cannot be
Fragile.
Faith
Must be tough.

It is not enough
As something
Quietly known.
Faith must be
Shown.

Life Contract

Thank You, Lord,
For never equivocating.
Your promises hold
No ifs, buts, or maybes;
No qualifying clauses,
No hidden loopholes.

Your Word
Is Truth
Without ending;
Never needs
Renewal or
Amending.

Perspective

Lord,
Sometimes we love
Other people so much
That we do not even
See their flaws.

That must be
How You love me!

New Beginnings

Lord,
Today a new baby
Was born into our family,
And looking fondly
Into that tiny,
Unprejudiced face,
Everything else
Gently falls
Into place
And I feel better
About the human race.

Grandmother

Each Sunday
She sits in the
Pew ahead of me,
So neatly dressed,
Her clean, white hair
Coiled into an
Old-fashioned bun.

Her clothes are
Crisply pressed
And only her face
Is lined,
But her faith
Shines through with
The patina of
Old silver,
Seven times
Refined.

TIME OUT

Medical Report

This man
In his stiff white coat
Is not telling me
What I want to hear!

He is not saying
That all is well
And that I have
Nothing to fear.

Instead, he is
Hurling words at me
That boil down
To this:
Something is
Very much amiss!

Lord,
As You have before,
Help me once more!

55

Entering the Hospital

You know, Lord,
This was not my idea!
I have been stamped,
Tagged, processed,
And been given a number.

The nurses try to relieve
The impersonality
By calling me by name
(After looking at my wrist tag)
As if they really know me.

But they do not know me.
They do not know
That I forgot to sew
The button on my husband's good shirt,
And that he will wear it anyway,
When he goes to church,
Without me.

They do not know
That the miniature rose
I have been coddling
Will bloom and fade
Before I see it again.

They do not know
How frightened I am!

Lord, I cling to
My one certainty:
That I am more than
A number on Your list,
And that You will remain
Beside me each minute
And will call me by name
Without having to look
At the tag on my wrist.

Surgery

They wake me at dawn
For the last-minute
Medication.

I give myself over
To science and
Technical instruments
Without hesitation.

In that nether world
Which I now enter
I know that You
Are at the control center.

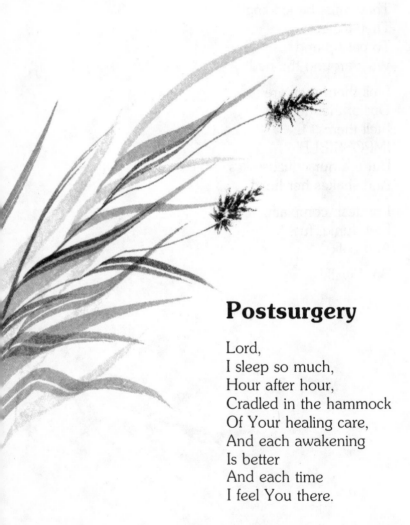

Postsurgery

Lord,
I sleep so much,
Hour after hour,
Cradled in the hammock
Of Your healing care,
And each awakening
Is better
And each time
I feel You there.

Second Day

They must be kidding!
They expect me
To get up and
Walk around the bed!

I tell them they are
Out of their minds!
I tell them it is
IMPOSSIBLE!
But the nurse just smiles
And shakes her head.

I protest, complain,
Fret, fume, fuss
And balk

But I walk!

Visiting Hours

He comes so loyally,
This good husband of mine,
So determinedly cheery
In his unironed shirt,
But I see lines of worry
Around his mouth,
And his eyes
Look weary.

Lord,
When he is here
That little while,
Help me to smile.

24-Hour Care

Lord,
Do You never rest?

No matter what
Dark hour I awaken
And call on You
For encouragement
And a spiritual lift,

There You are,
Working the
All-night shift.

Shadow

Lord,
Last night
You reached down
And took the woman
In the bed next to me.

She was very ill,
But we had talked,
As women do who have walked
In the valley.
She told me
She was not afraid
To die.

Lord,
Was she more ready
Than I?

The Physician

Lord,
I am forever grateful
For the way You heal
The wounds of
Body and soul.
How gently You
Bandage and
Patch me.

And when I am close
To falling from grace,
You are always there,
Ready to catch me!

Hospital Meals

Lord,
I really try to be
A good patient,
Not cranky or demanding.

Perhaps I could be
Less crotchety, though,
And maybe even more mellow,
If I found something
On my tray besides
Jello!

Discharge Day

Lord,
Thank You for this
Wonderful healing,
For this unbelievable,
Delirious feeling
Of going home!

(And none too soon,
Because my husband is
Beginning to look
A little ragtag.)
I think he must have
Got into the
Thrift-shop bag.

Homecoming

Oh, Lord!
I am so thankful
To be home again!
The house looks so
Beautiful and warm,
Colors seem brighter,
Every stick of furniture
So familiar and precious,
With my beloved family
Waiting.
How could I ever
Have thought
The place needed
Redecorating?

TIME OFF

Mountain Weekend

We were tired,
Needed a break,
Needed a vacation,
Needed to get away.

And You provided
This marvelous retreat,
This nourishing, healing
Interval of rest.

You, who never
Take off so much as
One day!

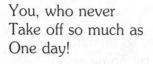

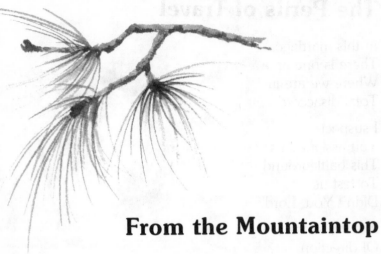

From the Mountaintop

Up here,
Where pine scent
Does not come
From a spray can
And the sun
Does not have to fight
Its way through smog,
We shed the
False veneer
Of city streets,
Take a deep breath,
And thankfully renew
Our pledge to You.

Priorities are clear
Up here.

The Perils of Travel

In this marriage,
There is one area
Where we are in
Total disaccord.

I suspect
You assigned us
This battleground
To test us,
Didn't You, Lord?

It is my sense
Of direction,
Or lack of it,
And my inability to
Read a map.
I cannot seem
To get the knack of it.

I either have it
Upside down,
Or our route lies
Under the fold
And I miss a turn
And the signs are all
Greek to me

So that when we somehow
Arrive at our destination,
Tired, hungry, and cold,
My mate will no longer
Speak to me.

Coast Highway

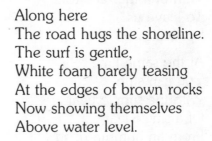

Along here
The road hugs the shoreline.
The surf is gentle,
White foam barely teasing
At the edges of brown rocks
Now showing themselves
Above water level.

We can see
Pelicans perching
Impassively on the tips.
They are wise to
The way of tides.
They know there is
Turbulence to come
But for now they doze
In the noon-bright sun,
Serenely in command.

Their home
Is not built on
Shifting sand.

71

Divine Palette

Lord,
Your artistry
Is beyond comprehension!

You create
The Grand Canyon
With one master stroke
To leave us
Speechless.

At the same time
You can stun
With the simple beauty
Of a single leaf
From an autumn-dyed
Oak.

Sunday Morning, Zion Canyon

We are a congregation
Of two
As we worship
At this altar
Of stillness.

Across the quiet stream
Brown-eyed deer
Pause at the
Water's edge,
Velvet ears twitching
In the cathedral silence.

They seem
As much aware
As we are
Of Your
Majestic presence.

Desert Interval

Out here in this
Clear and uncluttered space,
Away from answer phones
And computers,
Away from caramel corn
And politics . . .

Out here,
Where there is no place
For doubt and indecision,
Where values are honest
And rock-hard
And nature gets
Down to basics
And no-nonsense truths . . .

Out here
My faith is strengthened
And I reach summits
I cannot find within
City limits.

Flash Flood Area

It is not wise
To be in the desert
When the storms come.
Saguaros and Joshuas
Offer no protection.
Wind-rounded rocks
Give no shelter.
Verbena is washed away
And tumbleweeds
Lose their moorings
As the desert floor
Becomes a flowing river.

The storm is no giver
Of quarter or mercy
And all tiny creatures
Scurry deep underground.

Out here,
The rains don't
Fool around.

Along a New Freeway

From high
On a telephone post
The red-tailed hawk
Looks down on his ruined
Domain.

Men and machinery
Are tearing up
His hunting grounds,
Tall trees
Have toppled
And meadowlands
Are paved over.
No field mice remain.

Look, bird,
Don't worry!
In spite of all
The frenzy and flurry
Of trespassing man,
God has a place for you
In His plan.

San Marcos Pass

Here in this green canyon
Between mountainsides
Of chaparral and live oak
The land flattens out
Into quiet pastures.

Not five minutes
From the frantic freeway
Out of Santa Barbara,
Cattle browse peacefully
On meadow grass,
Birds call softly
And for a few miles
Our world returns
To rural simplicity.

Thank You, Lord,
For this brief remnant
Of serenity.

Sunset at Newport Beach

One evening
We sat on the cooling sand
And watched a school
Of playful dolphins
Put on an acrobatic show
Against the backdrop
Of a Pacific sunset.

Their sleek, dark bodies
Twisted and turned
In graceful leaps
While the sky reddened
Into fluorescent streaks.
As the last trace of sun
Sank into the horizon
And the house lights went down,
The performers swam away
And the heavens turned
All purple and bruised.

What an extravaganza,
Which only You, Lord,
Could have produced!

Act Three

Lord,
I do not like
The limelight,
Do not want
A starring role
In this great pageant
You set before us.

When the credits roll,
When all the actors
Have taken their
Curtain calls,
I just want to be listed
As a member
Of the chorus.

Final Word

Lord,
When I stop to think
About it
I am overwhelmed
By the enormity
Of my debt to You
For all my blessings
Beyond knowing
Or seeing.

All I can say is
Thank You, Lord
For just being!